NICK WARE

THIS PRESENT BEACH

FIERY HEDGE POETRY

1

THIS PRESENT BEACH

First published 2022 by Fiery Hedge Publications

ISBN 978-0-9930473-9-8

Cover design and photography by Nick Ware assisted by Lewes Epps

Printed by kindle direct publishing

For every copy sold, the price will include a £1 donation to Prostate Cancer UK

Nick Ware

THIS PRESENT BEACH

Contents

To my wife, Chris, to my children – Kathryn, Matthew and David – and to my grandchildren, Timothy and Guinevere, all sharers in and enrichers of these narratives; to the memory, also, of two mothers, Sheila Sparke and Gill Ware

I have in front of me the beautiful bunch of dahlias that you brought me yesterday; it reminds me of the lovely hour that I was able to have with you, and of the garden, and in general of how beautiful the world can be in these autumn days … All that is needed to bring that home to one is a few bright autumn flowers, the view from the cell window, and half an hour's 'exercise' in the prison yard, where there are, in fact, a few beautiful chestnut and lime trees. But in the last resort, for me at any rate, the 'world' consists of a few people whom I should like to see and be with. The occasional appearances of you and Maria, for a brief hour as though from a great distance, are really the thing for which and from which I principally live.
DIETRICH BONHOEFFER: LETTERS AND PAPERS FROM PRISON

The walls fall down, the doors blow open
And you are standing in the sun…
BETSY COOK/LINDA THOMPSON: ONE CLEAR MOMENT

THRESHOLDS

At the first door,
we stood and shivered in the porch,
dusted with snow, still wincing
at the night wind's unwholesome ministrations;
impatient, knocked
on unvarnished wood…

We waited, listened
for the slow and unhurried
approaching steps,
the sounds of movement
on the other side.

Curtain swish, rasping
bolts and the sigh
of an opening:
we were met, at once,
with kindlier airs;
inhaled wet earth smells, meadow scents.

The hall
was softly carpeted:
as we wandered down
its sumptuous aisle,
the door eased to behind.

*

The second
was already ajar
and scarcely remarked
for the light-filled room beyond.

The lifted window casements gave
upon vast estates:
we lingered for the views

between those sills and the far horizon –
ripening fields,
dense woodland,
ancient moor.

Shadows slid
over the inner walls:
swallow-shapes sweeping
the pathways of the sun,
wings caught
on the periphery of vision.

We ambled
across that shining space,
oblivious
of the steady tick
of time.

*

The third door
was garlanded with leaves, flowers, fruit –
their colours wearing
an end-of-the-afternoon
intensity.

We entered, conscious
of the sudden cold in the passageway,
but reached the parlour warmth it trespassed on:
the flickering hearth,
the homely table laden
with nature's bounteous best –
fresh loaves, rich stews,
their rising fragrance
gathering in the nostrils,
their flavours
elucidating on the tongue.

Partaking of such wealth,
we pushed back benches, raised
flagons to life;
replete, sat on and watched
mesmeric apparitions
in the flames.

*

Before the fourth door,
we hesitated,
feeling the creeping chill
of its keyhole
insinuations.

Unlatched, its claims
were substantiated
with icy truths:
stasis of garden, yard;
mist shrouding mouldering implements;
the air sleet-edged
with darkness welling up
in denuded lanes.

We climbed in shadow,
stood on the ridge, looked back
at the house we'd left diminishing below;
then staggered across
the vast, wind-pummelled heath –
beleaguered travellers,
minds intent
on a bare porch waiting
somewhere in the dawn.

FIRST DATES

1. MAXWELL'S

Other than the strolls, it would have been
the very first: the entrance off Queen Street
surprising me (not you) with its sudden
ascent, the stairs' reverberating beat

transporting us into America.
Or where it seemed, inside the burger joint
(hard rock, the image of a skyscraper) –
that ambience capturing the excitement

of young love. Nothing beside this mattered:
with patience, you guided me around
the menu; in due time, courses appeared.
We ate and talked, departed hand in hand.

The mint imperial offered at the till
scarcely increased the sweetness of the bill.

2. TWELFTH NIGHT

Which College staged it quite escapes me, now.
With nightfall, we'd headed for the city,
trusting that distance travelled would allow
the best chance of an anonymity

that Harcourt lacked. We were still "clandestine"
and – mindful of the subterfuge maintained –
smiled at the "kiss me, sweet and twenty" line:
behind closed doors, the bard's delicious hint

was hardly necessary. But the play
delivered, building true affection,
until that late moment of clarity:
all eyes were undeceived and we were shown

that difficulties in good time resolve,
how love will – in the end – declare itself.

WOMAN AND SUNDIAL, STRATFORD-UPON-AVON

Yes, it *was* posed: that shot of you –
leaning – the crook of one elbow
on the dial's edge as you check your watch
against the shadow's reckoning.

Late winter light honeys the stone
slabs over which *your* shadow slides
in the mild swelter of afternoon,
an unscheduled advance on spring.

We'd made the engagement official
the night before and marked the event
with an inaugural weekend
excursion. We were on the train,

that morning, with it all ahead:
Stratford and Shakespeare, marriage, children –
the day, the life, the sheer excitement
of the adventure we'd started on.

Nearly four decades lie between
the image and an older you
with whom I've shared that interval:
the girl's still recognisable,

still indisputably the one!
And – although years, now, hurtle by
(like the hours, then) – the same question
persists. Where, love, has the time gone?

APPROACHING MIDSUMMER, SN9

The heat, the heady greens and – at the bend –
the high-grassed verge obscures what lies beyond.
All week, my mornings orient me south
into Wiltshire's heartland, dense with summer growth
and sultry in the glut of summer weather.
Chalk downs wall in the skies that greet me there
among the lanes that intersect the Vale:
beneath the soaring cliff of Martinsell,
the undulations at Adam's Grave,
this other world – abundant, secretive –
closes around me, lures me on and in.
The green wave sweeps ahead, until the Plain
halts its advance with elevations
that hide the ancient magnet of the stones.
Inexorably, the days extend towards
the mid-year solstice. Travellers are on the roads.

June, 1989

REMEMBRANCE DAY

Not poppied, this one, the sward spattered red:
here, the earth's wound is staunched with daffodils,
their cheerful gauze circling this carapace
of soaring stone (early Cistercian)
islanded amid miles of carriageway
beside the doleful waters of the Aire.

Easters ago, we visited this place,
wandered among the ruins, discovered
the various curiosities and quirks
of the museum opposite – the most
memorable, now, the coin-implemented
scheduling of the sentenced man's last hours.

The diorama finishes beneath
the guillotine, head neatly basketed.
Callous insensitivity of youth!
We played the scene over and over
with little recognition for the plight
of the victim, the despairing family.

Loss, though, can undermine such resilience,
scrape away that veneer of carelessness.
So, ambushes in time and geography
catch at the heart, this morning, and invoke
the presence of those earlier selves – with me
nineteen years older and you one year dead.

Kirkstall Abbey, Leeds – 20th April, 1993

ON THE RISE

Uphill, all week –
and mostly in wind and wet –
one way or another,
you got me to carry you,
slung in my arms
or straddling my shoulders,
the street itself
unremittingly alpine.

Cornwall off-season:
the cottage waterside
with parking on the headland –
you, your elder
sister, your mother and I,
the repeated haul
between the coal wharf
and St Saviour's Hill.

You seemed my lot
for those upward ventures
with Kathryn independent
and Mum weighed down
by an unborn younger sibling:
that circumstance
saw you allocated thus –
my natural burden.

Not that it troubled;
I willingly embraced
the necessity
that hoisted you aboard
your paternal transport,
held you aloft – guessed how
the love that lifted you
lifted me, also.

October, 1994

HIGH

Like the pink balloon
above your party hat,
you are still afloat –
buoyant and serene –
when I come to collect you.

Little man –
so much the part
with your waistcoat,
your elasticated tie –
how I envy

the joyful
delirium
that holds the curve
of your upturned mouth
all the journey home;

would longer yet,
were it in my gift
to bottle and store
this happy fizz,
this bubbling delight.

GRADUATION

Of course, the images
of celebration: marquees
installed in the Castle grounds,
those minglings in the mild
September evening air;

the dim Cathedral aisle,
that shouldering in ahead
of the ceremony – eyes
trained on the spot-lit stage
as we waited among the shadows.

And the motel, next morning:
the slant of swallows' wings
above the glass of the rooflights,
restive perambulations
on the world's departing winds.

Lincoln – September, 2016

AT THE FRENCHMAN'S GRAVE

It wasn't on
the itinerary
or even the radar:
that mid-afternoon
scramble uphill;
an impulsively
conducted venture
above and beyond
the official end
of the Mawddach Trail.

*

Behind the church
(a climb in itself),
we mounted steadily –
shelf on shelf –
up into the day,
past the origins
of The National Trust.
Strenuous research
for the interest
of those cryptic signs!

*

The Frenchman's Grave:
that presumption
of the knowledge lacked –
what defined the life
beside his racial
singularity,
the true impact
of this European

upon alien soil,
in obscurity.

*

We altered course
at the fingerpost,
enquirers
into the mystery
that it introduced –
walled on one side,
the other tree-shrouded,
its hidden way
narrow, hemmed in
with expectation –

*

and came up short
at the fence, the fall
towards the town's heart
(beyond, the swell
of the Irish Sea),
saw the stone engraved
with his history:
trouble, enterprise;
the contingencies
of the life well lived.

*

Monsieur Guyard,
the good Auguste:
idealist,
even visionary –
a man abjured
in his homeland, thought
subversive,

revolutionary.
Now, this burial plot
frames the narrative.

*

Fleeing the siege
of Paris, he
washed up on these shores,
recovering by
the patronage
of movers, shakers –
the common ground
they trod apparent
in grateful tenant,
in honoured friend.

*

His refuge: 2,
Rock Gardens. Thus,
this slope (cut
into terraces)
became the page
on which he wrote
nothing more true
than that late yield
on thin soil tilled
along the edge.

*

And the harvest – flowers,
herbs, vegetables –
nourished his neighbours
no less than him.
That generous impulse
would also tame

the birds: hawk, raven,
partakers of
the kindness shown,
this human love.

*

Would we welcome him
in this post-referendum
Britain? *His* life's
largely forgotten;
new fugitives –
viewed with suspicion –
make landfall daily,
crowd in. If they close
the Channel entirely,
what will we lose?

September, 2017

EMOTIONAL GEOGRAPHIC

We met and married
near Oxford, city
of spires and meadows,
streets and waterways:
place of encounter –
given the chance, I'd
wander among its
thoroughfares, again.

After this, Swindon's
sprawling environs,
employment, the home
we made: in its time,
railway town, housing
the engine works – on
that platform, the first
two children arrived.

Then, Exeter, still
the sojourn of choice:
the third child's birthplace,
circled by hills – twin
cathedral towers
presiding over
its civic descent
into tidal plain.

The future? Nothing's
decided. We mark
the onward progress
of children: the range
that their lives, their loves,
determine; how they
enlarge the map the
affections trace.

IN SCOTLAND

1. WIND FARM

I'm walking with my granddaughter along
the dirt tracks gravelled out over the peat
of Eaglesham Moor: above us, turbines slice
the atmosphere, converting swathes of air
into so much wattage via the triple blades
that feed the force they scythe into the Grid.

Her parents – with her brother – tramp ahead,
their footfall raising dust. Watching it swirl
about their ankles then converge on us,
I turn and mime with her the brief half-run
that's, more than once, amused while spurring on
across this landscape wild with whirligigs.

Again, she imitates; at two, perceives
the humour in my simulation
of urgency, smiles up at me and makes
something of an advance – there's spirit in
how wilfully she shakes off the mild infringement
that's ventured with her grandad's steadying arm.

As young as this, her independence shows!
Congenially, still, we march among
the soaring columns stationed on the heath,
hearing the constant cutting into wind
of welded steel repeat hypnotically,
its mantra eerily disquieting.

Her grandmother and I grew up with coal,
saw the delivery truck come idling down
familiar roads, the roughly-hefted payload
of grimy sacks reducing, house by house,
though – even at the time – perceptibly,
the industry was heading into trouble:

the power failures, the evenings
with winter circling in the restless dark
that lurked beyond the pools of candlelight;
then – in the Eighties – Thatcher and the civic
unrest that surfaced in the Miners' Strike;
thereafter, dwindling viability.

Earlier in the day, we were greeted
with views of turbines grafted in their scores
to hillsides north of Gretna, either side
of the motorway – urgency apparent in
the sweeping motions that punctuated
their dizzily compulsive semaphore.

South of the border, there's more quarrel with
such installations, how they offend
the topographies of whole neighbourhoods
with small return. But – here, where winds abound –
the argument's moved on and the balance
commands the skies of Scotland's central belt.

Last year, we visited the grandchildren
on the east coast of Norfolk – their first home,
if superseded in the months since then
by the move north. They're already at ease,
seemingly, in this new location:
the future's different for the journey

that's brought them here, its arsenal of weathers
harnessed for less destructive purposes
than hitherto. They'll grow up to the green
alternatives of their adopted country:
they'll sow the open courses of the breeze;
they'll reap the virtues of the hurricane.

26th May, 2018

2. HERITAGE PARK

They've cleaned up the main exhibits
at Summerlee: ironware and steel
gleam all around as the grandchildren
weave among them, innocent

of smuts and grime. Items engage
or otherwise with small regard
for history: theirs, here, reaches back
no further than the first visit

and – of the things recalled – the best's
the tram in the museum yard,
enticing with its clatter-clang.
Expectantly, they climb aboard

and sit tight for the jolt that sends
them swaying off over the track,
delighting in sound and movement,
until they're stopped short at the fence

between them and the modern line
where sleek electric units chase
times of arrival. They alight,
glance in at the interiors

of terraced houses that depict
the home in different periods
of the industrial age, even
decades remembered by the adults

who shepherd them, keeping in check
their more unruly impulses.
Then, it's the tram, again, before
the homeward run. Perhaps, the day

redeems the nation’s dirty past
for them: that dubious legacy
will cloud their future, nonetheless.
How late we glimpse the urgency!

29th May, 2018

DRINKING IT IN

The moon,
a buoyant
lemon wedge

in cola skies
that effervesce
with stars.

29th October, 2018

A WIFE'S WAKE

Uncoupled
and unaccustomed
to the sharp exposure
of singleness,

the suited widower
stands at the door
for the parting words
of consolation

that leave him, hovering –
like the groom
at a wedding,
looking round for his bride.

NEW YEAR

What you envisage is this clearing sky,
this suddenness of sunlight – its kindling
with warmth of pale winter horizons
(the bare hills, graceful tree-skeletons) –
and, simultaneously, an unclouding
of the interior world in clemency.

You scarcely think the instant will arrive,
so rarely does the morning integrate
the soul and its environs: old griefs spill
over onto the day's clean sheet while, still,
you grasp at what might yet inaugurate
that better person, that more tranquil life.

CORTÈGE

in memoriam Sheila Myrtle, b. 9th September, 1926 – d. 21st December, 2018

In those last months,
when anxiety (ever
your constant) curbed even
the most ordinary of pleasures,
few things improved
upon easing you into the car
and squandering time
among the Devon lanes.

The mere sight of green hills
distracted, lightened:
you mused upon the fields,
the season's repertoire.
Somehow, the sense of motion
settled your agitation,
soothed that predisposition
for restlessness.

So, as the limousines rolled
downhill behind the hearse
then accelerated
into the traffic swell
of the A380,
we saw the Haldon ridge
suffused in winter sunlight
and could only suppose
you'd have loved the journey.

OWNING IT

There's always the dog
that I didn't want
and – annoyingly –
considers me God.

Importunate and
without shame or guile,
he imposes, makes
incessant demands:

exercise, meals or
attention. I'm
stubborn, ignore his
petitioning;

have him wait until
I decide it's time
or the need warrants
it. Walks are the best:

him with his head down,
rummaging networks
of scents in the field,
nostril-led trails; me

strolling, untroubled,
alone with my thoughts.
If he doesn't roll,
both return happy.

ALL TALK

I sometimes think the soul
is the conversation
the self makes with itself –
the continual,
internal dialogue
that arrests or sanctions
impulse, governs
inclination
or excuses it.

The murmurs sift and weigh,
questioning motive;
with luck, will narrow
the concerning distance
that separates what I am
and wish I was.

MEDICINE MAN

Colin delivers for the pharmacy.
The van's a common sight about the town
and bears the scars of ill-judged interplay
with gates and walls in thoroughfares laid down

with no thought for the future prevalence
of the combustion engine. In the main,
Colin directs his wheels with competence:
it's when he's pressed that – sometimes – things happen.

Nevertheless, he's good with customers,
makes nothing of the regular delay
in answering. Ever welcome at their doors,
he handles their concerns delicately.

They like him for his reassuring smile,
the gentle wit displayed, the unruffled
in-any-weather service. They mumble
their thanks and warn him: "Don't," they say, "get old."

*

It's the hands
that he notices:

the puffy digits,
the opaque skin

and the veins,
like wires afloat

in the surgical gloves
that receive his pen;

these and the tremors
that impede and skew

their initials, warp
into hieroglyphs

names with which –
incrementally –

they sign away
their depleting lives.

*

In snatches, mostly, on the radio,
he hears – between calls – songs, items of news;
how inescapably statistics show
the strains that longer living will impose

on services, upon society.
Colin, though, sees the truth: that future's here –
the demographic time-bomb's already
exploded, the tsunami's swept over

the human landscape where his vehicle
negotiates the devastation,
its hold piled high with pharmaceutical
relief, help for the casualties strewn

around an ever-widening catchment.
The Non-Stop Oldies are on Two, once more:
wryly, he notes that things look different
the *other* side of "When I'm Sixty-Four".

*

They're old, now,
look frailer each time
he delivers the pills
that alleviate
yet never wholly cure
their afflictions.

But the amorous candour
of the statuary
in their front garden
still intimates
the vigour of the passion
that seized them, once:

naked, they stand –
young man, young woman –
embracing, mouth on mouth
and thigh on thigh,
the bare flesh ripe
for beatitude.

And this current state
of companionship
in shared infirmity
speaks of enduring
mutual tenderness.
And of vows made good.

*

"Sweetheart!" "My lover!" "Darling!" These are some
of the most common appellations
that female patients reserve for him.
With men, there's more natural reticence,

but “Boss” and “Sir” imply their true respect,
“Dear fellow” the affection that they’d hide.
He – for the seconds that they interact –
would hardly think the fondness justified.

Not that he’s gauche or unappreciative –
simply uneasy with inflated worth.
“Angel!” “My saviour!” Colin’s dismissive:
that measured self-appraisal keeps the earth

firmly beneath his feet. He does his best.
Anyone would. He’s not remarkable.
Despite the doorstep praise, he’s happiest
with an uncomplicated “Morning, Col!”

*

Waving him down
in the precinct
of the sheltered complex,
there’s an elderly woman –
unkempt, wild-eyed –
who implores his help:
“This,” she shouts, “isn’t home!
I don’t live here!
I wish, *please*, to go home!”

It’s the man arriving
beside her who steps in:
“My wife,” he ventures,
by way of explanation,
“suffers with Alzheimer’s.”
That he, too, suffers
an elbow in the ribs
received for his trouble
duly confirms.

Still irked, she resists
his reasoning, heads
down the nearest walk
with him in anxious tow.
The property
nearest the exit warns
of the trials of age:
the nameplate bears
this legend – *Fortitude*.

*

He passes houses that he no longer
visits, where – now – no medicine will serve
the needs that readily dispatched him there
or put off the event that none may swerve

indefinitely. The "SOLD" sign at the gate,
successive skips, supply trucks, fitters' vans –
over ensuing months – will dissipate
what substance of the life recalled remains:

Brian, left winger in the lower leagues
during the Sixties (two goals with Carlisle);
Gina, who sat alone among antiques
obtained when new; Wilf, whose invariable

delight with calls somehow affirmed the role
that haunts his working days... Year upon year
sees them increase – the names of ghosts that travel
behind him in the dark interior.

*

The Grange isn't
the house that it was –
warm, prosperous,
ordered, well maintained.

Shabby, it stands
among waist high weeds,
slates missing,
the stucco ruined.

The glory, once,
of the neighbourhood,
The Grange isn't
the house that it was.

Mallory isn't
the man that he was –
handsome, witty,
self-assured.

Grunting, unfastens
the heavy door,
looks forth blankly,
his breathing laboured.

The pride, once,
of the neighbourhood,
Mallory isn't
the man that he was.

*

"Hello, young man!" It isn't irony
that frames the greeting: in comparison
with most in his domain professionally,
doubtless, he will appear the tender one.

This notwithstanding, he's beyond his prime
(retirement's scheduled in the next decade.)
From visages more senior in time,
he's learnt the road – there's harsh terrain ahead!

Yet, if he's lucky with his health, there'll be
pleasanter realms before the stumbling ground –
those long vacations in Tuscany
or on the Algarve. In the meantime, the round

distracts, demands Colin's attention,
steals more of the uncertain interim
until the day when he needs medicine
and someone else delivers it – to him.

SUMMER SATURDAY, ARGYLL AND BUTE

Coming down into Oban
that afternoon,

we saw the blue and white
of the marchers' ensigns

unfurl over the streets
above the Firth.

Purposefully,
they made their descent,

converged around the shops
on the harbourside,

their aspirations
immediately

discernible:
the colours were enough

for the visitors
departing for the Isles.

As the ferry left,
the shore was still astir –

as though the nation
might set sail itself.

15th June, 2019

ON THE BEACH

Guinevere's at the tideline:
planting wellies, stoops
and meets the incoming wave,
hand round the bucket tilted
into the shimmering crystal
slap of Atlantic swell.

She straightens, skimming off
a measure of that clear
elixir, then retreats,
decanting it among
the holes *we* excavate
and the silt closes up.

Timothy's crouched, intent:
his fingers probe wet sand,
emerging darkly crumbed
and sticky. The salt water
will wash it off, wash away even
the prints he's left behind.

Nothing we do will last!
The ledges round the bay
reveal how high the land –
how high the sea – once stood
and speak of the vast trauma
that shaped this present beach.

Here we are, though, alive
and tipping into joy:
the children at their play,
the adults tentative
but learning to accept
its gift – the transitory.

Calgary, Isle of Mull – 16th June, 2019

IONA

Between ferries, not time enough
to absorb its timelessness: the sense
of those in other centuries

whose landfall there made it their home
in exile or whose sojourning
inspired trajectories that lit

the far edge of the Great Whin Sill.
Yet – like those settlements of grace –
the memories keep their source in view

and see it manifest itself
in the mind's eye, on that inner skyline:
white sands, grey abbey, one green hill.

AMONG THE HEBRIDES

The hills hem
these sea roads: dolphins

erupt, astonish,
enthral the eyes

over glistening arcs
of iridescence.

The islands wait
on the far horizon,

biding their time –
like fabulous beasts.

Isle of Staffa – 21st June, 2019

BORDER COUNTRY

1. IN THE CHEVIOTS

That sense of transition: the uplands
visibly wilder as we headed down
the last road before the holiday let.
By Powburn, we were east of the high fence
they put between parts of the Union;
turning aside, we settled at their feet.

Emerging (after watching England win
against Sweden), we ambled up the hill
behind the cottage; on the level, found
the first Pele Tower of the several seen
across the county – standing sentinel
above the lane, the houses, the farmland.

The next day, we encountered another –
some miles off the A1, towards the coast,
in woodland gardens. Inside, we mounted
the ladders lifted by the householder
into the upper storeys and supposed
safety amid the perils of the raid.

Fear governed in those depredations
north or south of the border, never mind
the allegiances of the victims
picked off with scant respect for national lines:
theft and abduction, if unsanctioned,
were customary evils of the times.

Up on the roof, the views on every side
were variously calm and untroubled,
the sense of menace curbed entirely since
the violence of the reivers dissipated.
In that knowledge, we ventured unassailed –
the same week – into Scotland, more than once.

And stopped, *once*, passing over Carter Bar,
for the obligatory pictures on
the boundary, the upright marker stones
arresting travel by the aperture
that penetrates the hills, direction
inscribed above your image on the lens.

The Lowlands half in shadow – radiance
lighting the Pentland Hills, the Lammermuirs –
we stood and gazed upon the evening side
of the tall ridge between two regions
defined less by themselves than their neighbours,
how they approach this natural divide.

7th-14th July, 2018

2. AT THE ROMAN FORT, BIRDOSWALD

Either way, miles of wall
straddling this northern fell,
though nothing like the height –
this many centuries on –
that once confronted tribes
living beyond the pale
of empire.

Wandering around,
we picture how things stood
(the former garrison,
traces of settlement
under its watchful might):
learn how the Dacian cohorts
deployed here in their day
left homes in southern Europe
and earned their livelihoods
holding Rome's borderline.

The tribune, Julianus,
buried his infant son
among these fields, recording
the hurt with words on stone
translated since and apt –
given these rancorous times –
for their foreign perspective:
the bureaucrat and soldier
remembering his dead
with all this land's deceased,
whose union in the earth
confused their destinies.

14th October, 2018

3. VARIATION ON AN AL STEWART THEME

Piano rumble – low – the riff
building at speed; Moog strains then bass
jarring beneath; Al's measured voice
developing his narrative
with images of contraband
and shifting tides, the moon and wind.

I heard it on the radio
for the first time four decades back
and, still – when listening – the track
disturbs the given status quo,
its tone and tempo edgier
for Peter White's Spanish guitar.

The elements, the altered maps;
word, ever, of insurgency –
here, rituals lose their potency,
worn down with empire's slow collapse,
while, deftly, trademark Stewart rhymes
disclose the zeitgeist of those times.

The intervening years compound
these states of turmoil and unrest:
the convoys of the dispossessed,
the armed usurpers of their land;
hardening political debate;
the nourished fear, the fostered hate.

Things come apart: old certainties
dissolve; the vehement pursue
their end, impose their favoured view.
No less than in the Seventies
(catastrophe or new world order),
we're on the cusp – we're on the border.

4. RETROSPECTIVE

"And walls come down..." Ingenuous opening
of the intended sonnet that never
progressed. November, 1989:
Berlin had the attention of a world
astounded into hope by the events
unfolding on its streets as citizens
defied their separating infrastructure.

A smaller revolution had begun
the sixth week in of that momentous year
with early tremors on the labour ward
prefacing wonder at the seismic change
they signified – in me, in mine, in how
thereafter life routinely shaped itself
around the tender incomer's demands.

The spectacle, months on, of those crossings –
the ruptured line dividing East and West –
informed my meditations on the state
of the planet, on the prospects of the child,
given that these developments fulfilled
their heady promises of openness
and ideologies in dialogue.

With guarded optimism, we embraced
that future for the February girl:
we watched her find her feet, reach for the sun,
imagined how the earth – for her – would prove
the better for this sudden transcendence
of present borders, for this empathy
with others met on their opposing sides.

Instead, we saw the lumbering fighter planes,
bound for the Gulf, win clear above the downs –
impending storm clouds troubling the distant
horizon. Bulletin by bulletin,
alarm increased that escalation
might spark off some kind of Armageddon.
As it was, we were spared the burning rain.

Life went on, pleasant domesticity
prevailed: wars happened in the background, fear
diminished, joys intensified, until –
with 9/11 – the presumption
of safety crumbled. Terror in the midst,
that furtive danger would accompany
my little daughter into adulthood.

This last year, we've observed two thirtieths –
her birthday and the anniversary
of the East German wall's destruction.
If anything, the era since the fall
has witnessed *more* attrition – enough
that (in some quarters) walls are back in vogue,
help promulgate the hostile boundary.

The sonnet was abandoned. In the day,
I'd thought *"Remember Troy"* the fitting end,
allowing some ambivalence. Beyond
clashes of nationality or creed,
my eldest child – the mother, now, of two –
like millions on this orbit of the sun,
creates anew the home, the family.

December, 2019

NATIVITY

Again, with Christmas, we assemble
the crib set, organise the scene:
God's family lodged beneath that humble
roof – quite improbably serene –
with various beasts traditional
around the infant in the stall.

The timescales of the versions differ,
however they're interpreted:
in truth, shepherds and magi never
rubbed shoulders in that musty shed,
arriving months or years apart
and mingling, now, only in art.

Still, we perpetuate the fiction
that neatly houses both at once,
that views with seasonal affection
the sight of kingly aliens
beside rough locals – rustic, sage,
on that first night, on that same stage.

It's the humanity we cherish
in this amalgam of events,
the hope these disparate figures nourish:
beguiled by their euphoric stance,
we sense in its economy
welcome and inclusivity.

Above this city, swathes of neon
obscure the seraphim, the star:
their message of accommodation
carries, though, on its murky air,
as wistful sceptics are undone.
Surrender. Make what peace they can.

FOR THE CHILDREN

And we gave them so much;
gave for the joy
that lit their faces
hours before dawn.

Now, the excitement fades,
like the afternoon,
and they sink – exhausted –
among scattered marvels.

That the generous impulse
worked largely with our own
weighs on the soul:
as the night descends,

we picture orphans,
the gaunt survivors
of genocide, famine –
eyes dull, expressionless,

in the arid state
they've inherited.
And, of sober mind,
we imagine Christmas

afresh, with gifts
at once more mundane
and more spectacular
than these novelties –

with shelter, warmth,
nourishment, medicine,
enduring kindness
and the end of war.

BREXIT POEM

Four nations divided:
to go or to stay!
The English decided –
well, are we UK?

1st February, 2020

COOL ASSASSIN

Spring in the offing,
the end-of-winter wind
stalks the countryside,
slashing at will with its knife.

February, 2020

ON ST DAVID'S DAY

And I will praise the early daffodil:
heraldic, it stands, ahead of its season,
weathering wind and storm and bitter hail;
with cheerful grace, usurping chilly ground.

And I will praise the steadfastness of men
who, six whole days, laboured beneath the earth
and – on the seventh – sang revival hymns,
the chapel-windowed light transfiguring them.

And I will praise the hope that lives within
what salves the eyes and ears and moves the heart;
that, from the depths, emancipated song
and – over wintry miles – imagines spring.

PANDEMIC SPRING

Late March and the birds
are upping the volume
for their morning chorus.

The light makes its appearance
earlier in the day,
remains noticeably longer.

Defiant daffs crowd
onto avenues, cluster
sociably around village greens.

Ubiquitous and unrestrained,
spring shows its hand:
the abundance spreads

with potent disregard
for humanity's
near-hibernation.

LOCKDOWN WITH EDWARD THOMAS

Most years, about this time (since the first time
I opened it), that book comes off the shelf:
the singular account that only you
could give of eight days' travel, cycling west
at Easter – the anticipated war
sixteen months off. At once, I'm on the roads
(denied, now, by constraints of geography
and current social rules for public health) –
no few familiar, like the Tillingbourne's
companion on its course below the downs
that naturalised my adolescent self.

In Wiltshire, it's more what you skirt around
that resonates: the names of villages
on the circumference of the Pewsey Vale
recall that centre and my countrified
daily commute while serving at its school.
Keeping with you along that boundary
affords me Trowbridge, Melksham and – among
those neighbourhoods – perhaps the sublimest
of passages (before the finale),
describing joy in motion and the scenes
about you on that Monday afternoon
when all seemed radiant, so ethereal
you could envisage such an afterlife.

So much of what you documented, then,
has vanished in the century and more
that's passed over the landscapes visited.
Doubtless, you'd mourn the absence of the elm,
find things adversely altered or erased
completely, but the roads themselves remain:
narrow or wide, straight or meandering,
they shepherd traffic, shoulder memories.
Unquestionably, you'd still recognise
parts of the Fosse – Downside, Nettlebridge's

decline, the steep escarpment of the Mendips –
and, more than business parks or industry
where meadows stood, you'd hate this curtailment
of movement other than the functional.
That spring will come, we're certain, but there's no
meeting it in advance by venturing
those distant highways – we'll await it, here,
with you and your persuasive quest in mind.

So, yes – in this "unprecedented" year –
I'm travelling, once more, vicariously
between the suburbs and the sea at Kilve,
intent upon the culmination
over the southern Quantocks with its views
around the compass, stretching into Wales.
It's on those slopes I'll meet you, once we're done
with lockdowns; but, for now, your words admit
the earth, the fields, the hills, the open sky,
rain, sun and wind, superbly manifest.
The first-day purchase of the Other Man
(your alter ego), I'm that bird – released.

April, 2020

VIA DOLOROSA

Well, here you are
on that final road,
paved with malevolence –
surely the hardest yet.

And the destination –
not one that inspires
or, in some way, makes
the journey bearable.

Lord, here we are:
up close and all too personal,
hemming you in,
crossing your onward path.

The angels watch:
cry and they'll intervene –
one word and this ends.
Are we worth it, after all?

INCARNATE

Inimitable God,
quietly slipping in
among your creatures, incognito;
standing in the same skin,
inhabiting their humdrum.

Indomitable God,
at war with easy faith;
posing the salient question,
venturing awkward truths;
persistent, difficult.

Inestimable God,
one with us in the pain,
your arms stretched on the cross –
its strained arithmetic
the measure of your love.

SWALLOWS, EARLY SUMMER

It’s that high-pitched
babble along the lines

between telegraph poles
or the slalom sweep

of wings overhead
that makes you aware

that they’re back among us,
owning the air –

as if they’d never left.
They’ll patch old nests with mud,

will multiply
as the days increase:

gypsies, transients,
they’ve mastered the art

of smuggling themselves
past border control,

of evading customs.
Traversing seas,

appropriating winds
on their ravaged path,

they materialise
in the neighbourhood,

betraying nothing
of those vagrant weeks;

assimilate
without a second thought,

belonging – as the season,
while it's here.

THIS TIME LAST YEAR

This time last year,
we were on the ferry,
heading into the Firth.

This time last year,
we watched as the mainland
slowly receded, distanced itself.

This time last year,
Mull's wild Atlantic coast
was unprecedented.

This time last year,
we were isolating
with the grandchildren.

June, 2020

COURIER, 2020

Invariably suspected
of carrying something other
than the regular packages,
you mask and glove up, approach,
knock at the door, lower
the parcel onto the step,
withdraw; at a comfortable distance,
watch as the faces rise –
like fish – towards lounge windows,
smile and wave, evidence
the life revolving dimly
behind aquarium glass.

IN A TIME OF PANDEMIC

Parted, we miss embrace:
speech carries over space;
is touching, nonetheless.

THE LONG VIEW

Eventually, we will have vaccines
that afford some measure
of immunity.

Eventually, we will lose
the unease that's still aroused
by the nearness of others.

Eventually, we will let
the masks slip, the smiles suspended
recover, return – full-faced.

Eventually, we will meet
the ones we've missed, embrace those
held dear in separation.

AT SLIMBRIDGE

We gaze out over abundant
meadowland east of the Severn,
river-fed pasture ruffled by
adrenal air. Ahead, we see
the lapwings rise, revolve, return,
sequence their soar and settle – their
black and white alternations
above the field. Elated, we
embrace the moment's uplift, catch
the happiness that meets the cast
and gather of their net of wind.

22nd August, 2020

UPTIGHT AT THE PROMS

Rule, Britannia! Britannia, rule the waves!
Let's forget that Britons ever trafficked slaves.

September, 2020

WILL NEVER HARM

Words are only the start:
repeated, hostile names
become labels, marking off
the carriers as those
of inferior or no worth.
The labels fasten, fix
perceptions, form the views
that shape the policies
that validate the means:
napalm, machete, gas,
machine-gun, cannon, spear,
arrow – or anything wielded
in anger – sticks and stones.
Words are only the start.

WHOOPS!

Nobody mentioned
the elephant in the room
(having been trampled!)

SERIOUSLY

In my youth, it was popular for jokes
to cite an English, Scots and Irish man:
with narratives devolving round these blokes,
the gags featured neither Welsh nor women.

The humour followed nationalistic tropes:
odds-on, the Scots were sour and miserly
or else inebriates; absurd mishaps
confirmed the Irish in stupidity.

Invariably, the English would display
their breeding; no ridiculous foibles
embarrassed the superiority
inferred over those Celtic marginals.

Encounters somewhat compromise the jest:
the Scots seem mostly generous and kind,
the Irish wise; women and Wales exist;
the English aren't more naturally refined.

Levity masks the deeper rivalries:
patterns of invasion and conquest
compounded into ideologies –
cultures derided, languages repressed.

However lightly we misrepresent
neighbours, the truth's ill-served in that the gaffe –
excused – maintains supposed entitlement:
with histories in the mix, who else will laugh?

CRUISE SHIPS OFF TEIGNMOUTH

Once, their itineraries were clear:
the sailings timed, the stops scheduled,
they crossed seas – each a moving world
above the night-reflecting deep.

With morning, now – daily – they keep
their stations on the horizon: those
mute giants stalled on the tide's silver;
marooned, like whales, in the shallows.

October, 2020

TEMPORARY RESIDENTS

The builders are in, so – mindful that the dog's
emphatically "on the spectrum" and courtesy
of some generous friends – the household's removed twelve
miles
and we're living by the coast in the bungalow
that Barry's parents once inhabited.
Décor that he remembers from his youth
evokes the penchants of the mid-Seventies:
walls coated in their anaglypta bark,
the ceiling an uneven canopy
of polystyrene tiles. Carpets and curtains
give off the stale odour of nicotine
from the same era. Since it was left to him,
Barry's come down with Edith and the kids
in the holidays, introduced them to his town's
peculiar delights – the pier, the Point, the back beach,
the looming mass of sandstone that's the Ness.
Working up-country, though, they've let things be:
the tired interior will have barely altered
in decades. Now retired, they've scheduled in
developments; they'll gut it and extend,
sell up in Hants, invest collateral
in the improvement of their Devon base –
next year, it's hoped, if things allow. Meanwhile,
it's what it is: during the month or so
we've called it *home*, it's served us well enough,
though home itself will have been differently
imagined and configured by the time
this sojourn's over and we're settling in,
our semi somewhat other than it was
and altogether more contemporary.

Weekdays, with work ahead, I'm up at six:
in darkness, navigate the dog downhill –
leaves deluging the lane, the sky above
a scatter of constellated sequins stitched

into emptiness. Shimmers across the bay
distinguish liners languishing between
the shore and the horizon – week on week,
illuminate their immobility.

At this hour, just *last* week, lamplight disclosed
the night's rough sleepers: two – one tented up
among the pillars of The Corinthian Yacht Club,
the other poorly billeted behind
the Perspex of the shelter on the Front,
both hearing the incessant shingle-shift
and sigh of the tide below. They've disappeared
with Lockdown Two's inception – at a guess,
they're housed, if only temporarily.
The measure's more expedient than kind:
most won't stay on, once the restrictions lift,
but roam the local byways, bedding down
with dusk wherever it sequesters them.

I think how it will seem returning home:
fresh paint, new flooring – the entire downstairs
transformed beyond recognition. Then, how we keep
that aspiration of the perfect house
imagined, though inevitably time
degrades the substance, sullies the ideal.
We'll live with it, attempt immaculate
then settle on the real home that's more true
and varies by design, with circumstance
or in the steady wear and tear of years:
never the palace we might wish and, yet,
wholly sufficient in the scheme of things.

November, 2020

ILLUMINATIONS

1. ADVENT

Candles – we light them,
spaced at intervals across
the presiding dark.

2. WINTER SOLSTICE

At the furthest point
of travel, the journey back
towards light begins.

3. CHRISTMAS

Are you with us in
our midnight, child – you whose life
lights humanity?

4. EPIPHANY

In darkness, yet, may
we carry within us what
light has been revealed.

STONE IN MY SHOE

It's the small thing that irks
and will not be dismissed,
it's the matter that lurks
near the end of the list,

what you wish hadn't been
and my lasting regret,
the immoderate scene
that embarrasses yet.

It's the cloud in the sky,
it's the invoice that's due,
it's the grit in your eye,
it's the stone in my shoe.

It's the trauma behind
and the ordeal ahead,
it's the snag in the mind
and the ghost in the shed,

the disparaging jests,
the critiques that annoy,
the unease that arrests
one's ascent into joy.

It's the incoming tide,
it's the scar on the view,
it's the thorn in your side,
it's the stone in my shoe.

It's the character stain,
it's the hurt that runs deep,
it's the night-long refrain
that encroaches on sleep,

the disquieting thought,
the reproaches that damn,
everything you were not,
the imposter I am.

It's the dark closing in,
it's the frame that's askew,
it's the itch on your skin,
it's the stone in my shoe.

MORNING, LATE JANUARY

How light returns – so much
the sooner and sweeter each day.

How we leave the house, birdsong
pouring over us in showers.

HELLO, DAD

Eight years gone,
yet you surface, still,
in the round pool
of the shaving mirror,
your mild expression
and wayward hair

reflecting back.
Time after time,
it's that morning trick
of the eyes, the mind,
that shows – all things reckoned –
how like you I am.

FAREWELL, EDWARD THOMAS

After the rain has fallen,
the old earth seems made new:
fields lie drenched, rivers swollen;
rinsed sunlight mends the view;
the branch and stem are shaken
and gardens are infused
with scents that only waken
off petals that are bruised.

After the storm of passion,
the lovers move apart:
between their lives, they fashion
the pathways of the heart
that keep the dear companion –
over the course they're on –
in mindful step and union,
together or alone.

After the light has faded,
the traveller finds his rest:
by the inn's warmth persuaded,
he halts – the evening guest –
yet, always, on the morrow,
sets off along the track
and, in the road's long furrow,
the buried days run back.

After the devastation –
war's human losses weighed –
comes that late distillation
in memories of the dead
that stir at skylarks singing,
meadow and winding lane,
bird-haunted hedgerows ringing,
sunlight that follows rain.

RESULTS DAY

The examination
was ordeal enough:
forensic, harsh,
your inner substance tried.

Now, you will hear
the analysis –
the call that soothes
or intensifies the alarm

when your long-term future
hangs in the balance
and it's cancer
that's awarded the grade.

FROM THE ISLE OF ARRAN

West of us, Kintyre
stops short of Ireland:

straining the eyes,
we catch the Antrim shore.

The ferry that's passing
will dock in Campbeltown –

south of its wake, Stranraer
is hazy, guessed-at,

somewhere off the end
of the Galloway hills.

Like jigsaw pieces
randomly scattered,

these disparate parts
of the Kingdom loom:

between them and around,
the Atlantic opens

its weight of water,
isolating strands

over kinship's margins,
stretching empathy

with distances that perplex –
this near, that far.

Kilmory – 18th July, 2021

WONDERLAND

Unlike Alice,
we arrive without preconceptions

or none that survive
the impact of the fall:

everything's strange
and the speed of incoming data

completely overwhelms
the processors.

We adapt in time,
accept things as they are,

assume that there's no
different reality,

however we speculate
or theorise.

At moments, even so,
we neither fit

the landscape
nor fully trust the alternatives

imagined – sense our smallness
and, yet, suppose

an overstepping
of the boundaries placed.

We engage mostly
with what's immediate –

what's loud, what's vivid
and unignorable

in this dimension.
But the mood will come

when it will, interrogate
the fabric, pry

beneath the surface,
receive nothing back

that integrates experience,
that resolves

the discrepancies:
beauty and violence –

the utter
incomprehensibility

of it all.

CANCER OF THE PROSTATE

1. ON GUARD

Curse of the male line
(father, grandfather, great-
grandfather), you were always
ahead of me up the road.

Now, with your "Come on, then",
an early diagnosis
equips me in the fight
they scarcely knew they had.

2. A WALNUT-SIZED GLAND

The irony wasn't lost:
that this small, if vital,
component
of the mechanism
that fosters life – breath –
could be the death.

3. GENERAL ANAESTHETIC

Efficient, chap.
Sharp and to the point.
We were introduced –
that firm grip on my arm! –
near doors that opened onto
the theatre of (my) inaction,
his bustling hangar
littered with instruments, dials.

Punctuated his work
with cheerful explanation:
I'd kept up well enough
(or so I thought), until –
somewhere in the middle –
I
 just
      be-
          gan
                nod-
                      ding…

4. CONSCIOUS DELIGHT

Last night, we discussed
funeral hymns,
Be Thou my Vision
my one imperative.

The first thought upon waking
in the Recovery Bay:
File that conversation –
I'm alive!

5. FROM THE SIDE WARD OF GOOD HOPE

Gulls fret the evening air
beyond the open window:

my view across the bed
frames the horizon ridge.

Immobile, here, I know
that home's the other side.

Would I could tread those hills,
gaze at the estuary!

6. THE COMPLEXION OF THINGS (AT THE TIME OF ASKING)

The colour of urine
was never my chosen
speciality.

Yet – with night bags and bags of time –
it has, nonetheless, become
requisite study.

I've watched its jet infuse
with stark and bloody hues
this perpetual flush.

Then, how the palette's sunk
until more Chenin Blanc
than rosé blush.

7. SLOW RELEASE

Back home, I've wrestled off
the hospital band
but not the memory of its cuff
around this right hand.

8. P(EE) FOR POEM

Emptying the catheter
(the umpteenth time in the day),
it seems there's nothing fitter
for pissing the time away.

9. NOTHING HEAVIER THAN A KETTLE

That's my measure,
the current extent
of what I may lift
while everything mends.

There's some latitude:
nowhere do they state
the capacity,
whether it's empty/full.

But there's no relish
for pushing boundaries:
during these early days,
I keep largely

within what's advised,
allowing myself
this unsolicited
exemption card,

though – given the doubt
(lightweight that I am) –
I'm arguably still good
for a cup of tea.

10. AN EXERCISE IN TRUST

I'm working my muscles:
the mind's as much
as those of the pelvic floor

(*they're* holding well –
it's mostly in the head
that conviction wavers!)

Daily, the same
exertions: flexing
the relevant neurons,

rehearsing self-control –
my uneasy thoughts
arresting over time,

as the brain permits
or stems the flow,
gains confidence in the flesh.

11. IMPACT STATEMENT

That the odds were good I won’t deny:
the assumed weight of probability
was with me. That said, the stakes were high
without statistical certainty.

Quite academic, of course, until
the hand you’re dealt forces the gamble
on procedure – on emerging whole
or mostly, largely, functional.

12. COMEBACK

There's been no big fanfare,
no rapturous press release,
sounding of the all-clear –
I'm just back at the crease

and getting on with life
(the job, domesticity),
clattering aside the stuff
that chance sticks over me.

It's as though I'd vanished,
was quietly atomised,
then (mildly astonished),
again, materialised –

seemingly as before,
though stitchwork scars across
the abdomen infer
that it was serious.

"You're looking well!" I'm told
by those I meet, it's true.
Not that everytning's settled:
it's still a challenged view

but looking viable,
now, for the longer lease,
this gift of time to heal,
recover by degrees.

MARTINS, EARLY AUTUMN

Something settled, assured,
in their movements –

those accomplished circuits
above the reservoir,

sunlight rippling
beneath the stir of wings.

On the moor, summer's
accumulated warmth

smoulders, intense
as the stored tinder

of memory
that awaits the match

or, perversely, rain.
Return next week

and the scene will lack
the vivacity

that these migrants lent,
though otherwise unchanged.

And we'll covet, in them,
the sky-serenity

that informs their being
and animates

the simple moment given:
here, now; then, gone.

Venford, Devon – September, 2021

BETTER

Above Bishop's Cleeve, I seat myself
at the picnic table, opposite
my wife and son, who've – with me – lived
the seven weeks since surgery

and borne the strain of its impact
on my investment in the home:
the dog-walks, early morning tea,
shopping, meals and vacuuming.

For their forbearance, the reward's
this foray east, this venturing
onto upland chalk. This first day in,
we've walked along the escarpment; glimpsed

the shining river's path below;
by The Ring's bearings, determined
the names of various peaks. We've paused
for refreshment, here, by the clubhouse: I'm

handing round pints of choice – they're on
the cider, both, and I'm chancing it
myself, unexpectedly at ease
after all these months. Above Bishop's Cleeve,

my worries lift, my life resets,
distilling in this smaller glass
my sense that things are on the up
and better – thankfully – by half.

AGE OF SAINTS

1. COLUMBA

Dove he was not: difficult Irishman,
certainly, with his high-born notions
of preferment, but profound repentance
secured the island and its station
in Alba's waters, seeded Albion
with gospel colonies whose influence
steadied the kingdom shifts and engagements,
tempered the sword's edge with compassion.

Sure, the old plagiarist was obdurate.
The *Life*, nevertheless, records how well
he loved his fellows; how the example
governed their daily round; how, that last night,
they mourned the loss but felt his worth and weight –
Iona's soldier, their Columcille.

2. AIDAN

Gentlest of men, companion of kings
and beggars' friend, he roamed the countryside,
treading the same rough paths that others trod,
learning their language by his wanderings;
simple and generous in his dealings
with all, gave amply of whatever good
his journeys rendered him; repudiated
the flames lit by the Mercians with his lungs.

Loyal himself, he left his rocky ledge,
kept with intention that eleven-day
vigil before the gates of treachery;
deployed his limbs with understated courage
and made an end of this world's pilgrimage,
delivering his treatise bodily.

3. CUTHBERT

Young man who set aside ambition
at Melrose, negotiating the eye
of the needle by that point of entry –
for him, real life began at seventeen
and (mindful of its inspiration)
maintained its course with wholesome industry,
until, embracing the extremity
of Inner Farne, he finally lay down.

The soul of kindness when alive, it's said
that – fearing the incursions of the Danes –
the monks who disinterred his last remains
found them in death completely undecayed,
as though the marvellous vindicated
the boy's resolve: that faith, that diligence.

GOODBYE, MUM

The last time that I saw you, it was in
the Home: you'd moved there just two days before
and were delighted with your window view
of the steeply rising bank, fat pigeons jostling
for purchase on the sagging telegraph line.

You smilingly supposed you'd crick your neck
with looking for the sky and yet it seemed
you'd sight of the good earth and April's best –
their sounds and scents infusing your new room,
the kiss of early summer on your cheek.

We chatted easily, were positive
regarding the future; thought, perhaps, there'd be –
among the residents – Polruan people.
The chefs ("two chaps") served meals of quality;
staff were attentive, cheerful; you were safe.

And sanguine, given the situation:
you'd weathered winter in the hospital
with an embargo on all visitors.
Imagining the genial months ahead,
I talked of who might make the journey down.

I said *I'd* visit. Often. Meant it. "What"
(you eyed me, quizzically) "about the bill
for this?" I settled that anxiety:
"It's all in hand!" Later, though: "Maybe, I'll
enjoy it here, but not for too long" (that

said wryly.) When departing, I hugged you
a second time – I wish I'd hugged you more!
In the event, that hug was your last hug,
not that some sense of this accompanied me
into the midday warmth of Polperro.

But there's a sweetness, Mum, in how you passed –
thankful for life, not bitter at the end –
your dear eyes closing on that light-filled room
swirling with memories of other springs
and things around you at their loveliest.

THE PASSING OF GIANTS

for John Ware (b. 2nd January, 1930 – d. 3rd March, 2013) and Gill Ware (b. 30th March, 1936 – d. 25th April, 2022)

Nine years apart but – collectively –
their deaths were like the passing of giants,
the hills left bare and the sky empty
of those silhouettes, my established constants.

I mount the slope, stand on the horizon,
feeling the unchecked winds peruse
the space that opens around one
who must live beyond their kindly shadows.

THIN PLACES

The abbey – glimpsed, waiting across the Sound.

That sense of the departed, treading the pilgrim path.

The north beach – desolate, beautiful.

The highest point of the climb, among clouds and islands.

The grass along the verge (those pale flowers picked by the
children.)

This pebble that I grasp with my left hand.

Notes on This Present Beach

Although virtually all the material in this collection was completed between 2018 and 2022, some of the poems were conceived – and seemingly abandoned – much earlier. Fortuitously, these recovered pieces fit the geological structuring of the content with many of the memories they document informing contemporary situations. More than in other volumes, I'm conscious of the political debate that's dominated the period of composition and the poems hopefully reflect something of the times that gave them shape. Where I've addressed the context directly, I trust that it's more in terms of questions arising than statements of opinion, even if my own allegiances are apparent.

Where indicated, dates refer to the events or experiences with which poems originated, not their time of completion. I'd thought of opening with *On the Beach*, this being the emotional key to the collection and the source of its title. In the end, though, chronology determined the ordering of poems other than the *Border Country* sequence (July, 2018 – December, 2019), sections of which overlap material on the Hebrides (June, 2019.)

The National Trust's official website was helpful in supplementing the visit described in *At the Frenchman's Grave* with information about the site. The story of my encounter with Auguste Guyard seemed worthy of attention, coming – as it did – within little more than twelve months of the Brexit vote. Doubtless, he roused some suspicion in *Victorian* England and Wales; however, the surviving impression of the man is one that certainly vindicates the confidence of patrons, not least the famous John Ruskin.

The *Medicine Man* sequence was composed with an awareness of the John Lees song of that title (on the album *Barclay James Harvest and Other Short Stories*), also the Ray Bradbury novel (*Something Wicked This Way Comes*) that inspired it. Given my employment at the time, there's some merit in my invoking the familiar literary disclaimer that resemblances perceived between those in the text and other individuals are entirely speculative. In truth, irrespective of Colin's virtues, it's the "concerning distance" with which *All Talk* ends that most epitomises me.

Lockdown with Edward Thomas references his *In Pursuit of Spring*. Over many years, it has been required reading for the spring months and the means of transcending (momentarily, anyway) the constraints of work. The significance of the liberty that it affords only increased during the pandemic of 2020 and I consider the resulting poem the best that I completed on that subject. I'm uncertain of the artistic value of others that I've included in this volume; they are, though, there for the record. The same may also be true of the pieces on my experience with cancer in the summer of 2021!

Fay Sampson's *Visions and Voyages* and Christopher Hull's *The Bamburgh Reredos* helpfully informed the visits to Iona and Lindisfarne that generated the content of *Age of Saints*.

As ever, I am thankful to my wife, Chris, who's seen most of these poems before anybody else and kindly tolerates my writing compulsion. I must, similarly, thank my daughter and fellow Fiery Hedge author, Kathryn Epps, with whom I've exchanged material over several years during which I've generated the content of one collection to her two (*Hope is Coming* and *Driving Through a Rainbow*.)

Some of the material in this volume has been published over the last year or two in magazines on the Indigo Dreams imprint (*Reach Poetry*, *Sarasvati* and *The Dawntreader*.) It is therefore important that I express my appreciation of their editors, Dawn Bauling and Ronnie Goodyer, for the encouragement their recognition has given me and their exceptional services generally to the poetry world. I'm thankful, likewise, for the generous comments of others in the Indigo Dreams community and, indeed, anyone kind enough to take an interest in my work.

Ultimately, it is how I make sense of things and saves on the therapy bills, but the notion that it is – at times, anyway – of value to others perhaps justifies that self-indulgence.

Fiery Hedge Publications

Fiery Hedge Information:

https://www.facebook.com/fieryhedgepoetry

www.fieryhedge.wordpress.com

Also by Nick Ware:

Perception of Light (November, 2014)

Subdued Anthems: Back Catalogue, Volume 1 (September, 2015)

Strange Courtry: Back Catalogue, Volume 2 (November, 2015)

The Beautiful Place (November, 2022)

Other Publications on the Fiery Hedge imprint:

Kathryn Epps, Hope Is Coming (February, 2021)

Kathryn Epps, Driving Through a Rainbow (April, 2022)

Printed in Great Britain
by Amazon

10704902R00068